For Pet Owners

The Magic of Music for Pets

How to Use Music for the Well-Being of Dogs, Cats and Horses

*To My favorite Veternarian
Merry Christmas
2007
Love
Mike*

Understanding the Hearing Sensitivities of Animals and the Value of Music in Your Pet's Environment

Janet Marlow, M.A.
Composer and Researcher

Human Dedication:
To my husband, Alan Brennan and our sons Colin and Ross

Animal Dedication:
To Osborn, Oliver and Rags

Acknowledgements

My appreciation to the following people for their support and encouragement to go *beyond the music*: Alan Brennan, Colin Brennan, Ross Brennan, Dana and Mel Toomey and Shalom, Nancy Stokes, Pamela Holick, LaMyra Haynes, Patti Moran, Susan Begasse, Margaret Hurst, Wendy Broeder, Hedda Von Goeben, Dr. Laura Carey, Dr. Mary G.Battista, Dr. Dale V. Atkins, Mary Pope Osborne and Will Osborne, Pat, Vicki and Julia Daly, Stephen Rekas, Susan Hannah, Lee's Stables, David and Barb Starbuck, Alan Landau and Dr. Anne C. Hermans. My special thanks to Taylor Johnson of T.H.E. Audio, for his master teaching in engineering and audio science and to Henry E. Heffner and Rickye S. Heffner for their research on Auditory Perceptions of Animals, Laboratory of Comparative Hearing, Department of Psychology, University of Toledo, Toledo, Ohio, U.S.A.

Edited by Stephen Rekas

Contents

Preface

Growing up as a child in New York, I walked several long city blocks from school to my apartment building. Very often on this route, the sound of tiny meows of kittens huddled together near the basements of buildings would ring in my musician's ears. Stopping to pinpoint the source of the sound with sparked enthusiasm, a kitten courageously made its way towards my soft-spoken calls. Hungry and homeless, it did not take me long to decide that this kitten was going to be given a home where I was going to give it the best care. My family's small apartment and my mother's extended arm pointing "out" sadly became a ritual as the seasons repeated this scenario. Each animal would win my heart and each time I would have to return it to the street. In those days there were no rescue organizations or town offices to call to place homeless animals.

One winter, the day before Christmas, a group of children about my age, came running up to me while I was walking home. In exasperation, they said that they had a puppy that their parent's wouldn't let them keep and begged me to take it. They lifted up to my view, a white puppy shivering in their arms. "Of course I can," I said. Certainly, a homeless puppy would be the winning event to achieve my greatest wish. I named him "Snowball". He lived with us until my parents were able to find him a home with a big yard and a loving family. Through the years, I held this experience in my heart. Once I had a home of my own, my family and I happily adopted many animals with open arms.

The journey of understanding animals and their responses to music began with my cat, Osborn. For fifteen years, my family and I were devoted caregivers to our black and white cat, which we adopted as a kitten from a rescue shelter. From the day that I brought Osborn home, he always gravitated to my side whenever I was practicing the guitar, composing or singing. I observed that wherever soft music was playing in our home, that was where Osborn could be found resting. One evening, when he was fifteen years old, Osborn went out into the night and was nowhere to be found although we whistled for him in our usual way. We sensed something was wrong. The next day, Osborn crawled his way to our front door. He had been seriously injured in our country woods.

He spent five days at the veterinary hospital, where the staff gave Osborn their full attention and care. I went there every day and sang to him to soothe his last days. I noticed that there was no music playing in the area where Osborn was being observed. After five days he passed away.

Soon after we ceremoniously buried Osborn, I fell deep into thought as to how music could be part of an animal's life. If music can provide a soothing environment for humans, then why can't it do the same for animals? My experience with Osborn provided the inspiration to create my *Relaxation Music for Dogs and Cats* CD series. Although I had already composed and recorded CDs for human enjoyment, given the way Osborn responded to soft volume levels and certain pitches, I knew there had to be a way to make music suitable for animals.

During several years of research, I sought out information in books and published studies on the auditory awareness of animals. As I began to understand and absorb what I was reading, I attempted to compose meditative music that I thought might benefit dogs and cats while they rested. Then I applied the science of acoustics to the music. With computer software programs measuring decibel and hertz levels, I developed a "digital recipe". The end result was music suited for a pet's auditory spectrum, music that would soothe and evoke a sense of calm in the animal. That is how I began my journey of combining my passion for music with my compassion for animals.

Osborn, the inspiration for the music

Introduction

Music is everywhere in our daily lives- playing in our offices, in stores while we shop, in elevators, on our cell phones, as well as in medical and dental offices. Sometimes obvious to us and sometimes not, music is broadcast in these environments to evoke certain human responses as part of the overall experience. Studies have shown that music permeating different environments will subtly influence behavior. For example, people will stay longer in a shop where pleasant music is playing. At rock concerts people are stimulated to move. Music is magical in this way. It can change the emotional mood of a person. Throughout history and today, live and recorded music has a significant place in our lives as human beings.

In the animal kingdom the senses of dogs, cats and horses are closely related to those of humans, so these pets especially can be affected by an enchanting musical ambience. That is why I have entitled this book *The Magic of Music for Pets*. The following pages offer fresh information and a new perspective on the hearing sensitivities of your pet. You will see that there are many uses of music as a tool for caregivers to assist in improving our pet's behavior and quality of life as we cohabitate with them.

Although I assume that your pets have been telling you all along what kind of music they like and what kind they do not like by staying in or leaving a room. Caring for and managing our pets' acoustic environment is a new way to enhance pet ownership.

How important is the sound system volume and tonality to our pet? Why should we provide music in our pet's environment?

Without their owners realizing it, subjecting pets to sounds that offend their sensitivities can be painful to an animal's ears and cause stress and anxiety. On the other hand, surrounding pets with music specific to their audio comfort zone soothes and calms them. As dogs, cats and horses are highly sensitive beings, appreciating their acute sensitivities to sound adds another dimension to understanding their well-being. In nature, an animal's instincts led by their senses enable them to survive in their environment. As domesticated pets, their instinct is to do the same. For their owners, the use of music can be an effective tool to help pets in this regard.

Consider how rapidly the values of pet ownership have advanced in our lifetime. Animals are no longer regarded as just backyard pets. In a few decades, dogs and cats have gone from being used purely as mouse catchers and hunting companions or watchdogs, or from being used as scrap eaters at the table, to eating canned and holistic foods, sharing our beds, and being loved and cared for as family members in our homes.

Their world is no longer socially confined to our backyards or barns. They travel in our cars, they go for checkups at the veterinarian's office, they go to the groomers, they go on vacation with us, they wait for us in our homes while we are at work, we take them to work, some even have scheduled play dates and personal pet sitters. This is an amazingly fast social evolution for dogs and cats to have become such an important part of modern day life. Statistics provided by the American Pet Product Manufacturers Association, Inc. of Greenwich, Connecticut indicate that:

- 63% of U.S. households own a pet, which equates to 69.1 millions homes

- 45% of U.S. households own more than one pet

- In 1988, the first year the survey was conducted, 56% of U.S. households owned a pet as compared to the 63% in the present day

The approximate number of horses owned in the United States is 4.2 million. Pet owners spend billions of dollars on pets for veterinary care, food, grooming, vitamins, natural health treatments and boarding.

The level of care given to horses has also moved to a higher level, especially with the knowledge and use of holistic concepts. While researching equine environments, I discovered that many horse owners are becoming well versed in natural health remedies and cures. Equine magazines are filled with manufacturers' advertisements for hundreds of products for horses. The role of the horse has been changing too. They are no longer just farm workers used as plow horses or transportation, or to carry a soldier into battle; horses are now embraced as adopted animals in our home lives, saved from abuse and slaughter by rescue organizations and given sanctuary on retirement farms. The bond between man and horse is undergoing vast change in these ways, particularly in western culture.

Animals as well as humans feel the benefits of experiencing calm environments to promote good health. As our pet's lives more often parallel ours, we are beginning to utilize many of the same holistic practices for well-being. Horses, dogs, cats, and humans can benefit from massage, acupuncture, aroma and aqua therapies, organic diets, and now music designed for their hearing ranges. The acoustic care of pets, educating pet owners on the value of using music and spotlighting the significance of pet hearing sensibilities, is my effort to contribute to the expanding resources for the pet world. I believe that the new level of care that is now being given to animals is an inspiring and positive statement of our human progress.

Your pet's response to sounds and noises is an important way an animal can communicate its feelings about their world to you. Music is a holistic means of encouraging both a positive response to sound and pet behavior. Relaxation Music for Dogs and Cats, Relaxation Music for My Pet and Me, Relaxation Music for Horses for Equine Well-Being, and Relaxation Music for the Holidays for Pets and Pet Lovers comprises an evolving series of music CDs based on auditory sciences and specifically designed to elicit calm and positive behaviors in your dog, cat or horse.

How We Hear

Imagine that you are standing in the center of a field. The sounds common to this experience have an *aural perspective*, meaning that we hear in a 360-degree circle- the height and depth of all the sounds. For instance, one can hear the rustling of leaves in the trees, a breeze rushing past our ears, birds chirping nearby and in the distance, airplanes overhead, or cars on a nearby road; we can also hear the contrasting quiet of stillness. We identify these sounds as they occur by saying to ourselves, "I understand that is a bird, that is the wind in the trees, that is a car approaching, and that is a plane." Our reactions to these sounds are appropriate to how we identify the sound source in the aural perspective of our environment.

How They Hear

Dogs, cats and horses hear frequency ranges that are both much higher and much lower than what humans are capable of hearing. The important difference between their hearing capacity and ours is that an animal does not have the same spatial localization as a human, even though their hearing is more acute. In other words, they react to the sound and not to the sound source as we do.

If a truck with a loud engine roars passed us on a street, our human reaction is to identify where the sound is coming from and to evaluate whether the loud noise poses a danger. Dogs, cats and horses cannot spatially identify or locate the point of origin of a sound or frequency. For animals, this generates the survival reaction of fight or flight responses. Since our pets live in enclosed environments, these instinctive reactions to extreme sounds can often manifest themselves as behavioral responses such as stress, anxiety or aggression.

Have you wondered how your pet knows to alert you before there is a knock on your door? Why does a horse get agitated before any sign of a thunderstorm? Why does a cat gravitate to the quietest place in a room? Hearing is an active part of their survival instinct even in their domestic living quarters. Their senses are so acute, we have now witnessed animals fleeing from impending earthquakes or tsunamis, perhaps expressing a "sixth sense" according to H. D. Ratnayake, Deputy Director of Sri Lanka's Wildlife Department. Animals can be an alert system for us because their senses are not impeded by analytical thinking. As pet owners, we have a special relationship to our pets in this regard. There is a "sensory co-dependency" between our pets and us. We often rely on our pets' instincts to alert us, and our pets look to us to communicate back to them whether the event is "ok" or not.

Uniquely, the human brain, as it listens to music, can place the varying instruments in a spatial perspective while understanding the source of the sound as coming from a speaker, a stage, or the radio. Listening to music for humans is for the most part a one-dimensional experience. Trained musicians experience very detailed perception in being able to pick out a specific instrument at will in a three-dimensional spatial perspective.

Animals listen to sounds and music quite differently than humans. Your pet does not have the same audio/spatial localization ability that you have. If there are jarring sounds or shots at loud unexpected volumes, a dog, cat or horse will hear the sound at a greater intensity than humans. At the same time, they are not able to identify the location of the sound while feeling the jarring volume in their bodies. Dogs can react to a sound at .06 of a second. Now domesticated as co-habitants in our urban, suburban and country homes, we should be aware of their acute auditory senses. By all means, our pets need to play, run and exercise to remain healthy. It is also important to have an understanding of their auditory responses as we care for them.

For our pets, responses to low frequencies such as loud drums from a sound system can easily generate stress as it may mean, "Get ready to flee." For them, very low or very high frequency information and resonant vibrations are sounds that are indistinguishable from a loud vehicle or thunder. This uncertainty combined with the fact that they cannot locate the source of these vibrations causes them to react with their defense instincts.

The same can be said about feeling vibrations from stereo speakers positioned on the floor through their paws and bodies. Without having a carpet or non-conductive stand under the speaker to absorb low frequencies, vibrations are transferred directly to the floor surface as movement. This can cause distress. Understanding your pet from a subtle physical perspective will enhance your connection with its responses.

The human equivalent of a pet's auditory experience of sound in a home, kennel or barn is what can be called non-human psychoacoustic juxtaposition. This means that the sonic environment of your pet is experienced as a non-human, juxtaposed by your pet's level of psychophysical responses. To understand this, spend some time at the level that your pet lives, i.e., near the floor, to hear what your pet hears.

Fact: Not all breeds hear equally well; frequency response varies with the size of the specie's head plus ear size and placement. For this reason, the guiding principle behind the mastering process when recording music for pets is to center and compress the frequency range to the midpoint of the animal audio spectrum; that way the hearing capabilities and limits of a variety of breeds can be accommodated.

The Sound of Your Voice

Pets depend on the sound and inflection of your voice to understand what you want them to do. Have you noticed that you instinctively talk to your pet in a higher- pitched voice? Along with your body language, the higher pitch literally keys into your pet's hearing range. The fact that horses and humans have the most closely related hearing ranges underscores the amazing bond they have had for one another throughout history. The human voice is in a range that the horse hears comfortably.

Although animals learn to understand many words as commands for behaviors, the frequency at which you say the words is very important in how the communication is perceived. When I adopted Rags, he was already six years old. I observed that it took him about five months to fully learn the frequencies of my voice as his new caregiver.

Try the following experiment: Speak in different and extreme tones other than the natural speaking voice that your pet normally hears and see how he or she responds. Your pet may tilt its head in a quandary as to why you are changing your pet owner behavior! This is an easy way to see how animals respond to or "understand" our commands through their hearing range.

What is Sound?

The air around us is filled with the activity of the elements of sound. There is the volume of sound and noise, frequencies of sound and noise as well as the energy of electro-magnetic waves.

Imagine throwing a pebble into a still pond. Immediately, there is a ripple effect that starts from the center of the drop and reverberates in a circle further and further outward. Water is a conduit for vibration and the ripple effect of the pebble thrown into a pond closely resembles the way a sound wave pushes out into the air.

In our modern-day environment, invisible vibrations, frequencies and electromagnetic waves swirl all around us. For example, you may have observed your own reaction upon hearing the loud rumbling of a truck as it passed by you on the street. Your experience was not only taken in by your ear but also by your body. You cannot see the vibrations but you can certainly feel the truck's strong vibrations. The more intense the vibration, the more your body feels and reacts to it. High frequencies such as the screech of a car braking get our attention immediately because they are heard at the upper extremity of our range of hearing. Unlike our pets, however, we can mentally calm ourselves and our bodies with rational explanations. Such experiences are greatly magnified for our pets.

Although my dog Rags has heard our son practice drums in the basement many times, on hearing that first drum roll, Rags immediately seeks high ground at the opposite end of the house. His sensing of strong vibrations through the floor triggers a flee response.

Let's take a look at the common reference of the dog whistle. Francis Galton (1822-1911) was the first researcher to uncover facts about the range of frequencies heard by animals. He invented the dog whistle, also known as the silent whistle or Galton's whistle, used in training dogs. The dog whistle projects only one note, the frequency range of which is higher than the range of human hearing. Depending on the way the whistle is used, a trainer can attract a dog's attention for training purposes or even use it to inflict pain for behavior modification. The dog whistle is still used today. Regarding my CDs for pets, one of the questions I am frequently asked is, "Will I be able to hear the music?" I believe a general familiarity with the dog whistle accounts for this query.

In acoustics, the science of sound, sound is measured in terms of intensity or volume by decibels (db), frequency or highs and lows are measured in hertz (Hz) or cycles per second as well as wavelength, and the speed of sound is measured by the distance traveled per second. The hearing ranges and sensitivities of humans as well as dogs, cats and horses are measured in decibels (volume) and frequencies (hertz or cycles).

What is a decibel? A decibel is a numeric unit that measures and describes volume of sound. The numerical value of one decibel is equal to the smallest change in volume of sound that the normal human ear can detect. The term decibel is derived from the prefix deci-signifying the power of the 10th measuring intensity, and the suffix -bel after the inventor and developer of telecommunications, Alexander Graham Bell (1847-1922).

Here are some examples of measured decibel ranges. The maximum level for rock music is 150 db, a normal piano level is 70db; normal speech is 60db and a soft whisper is 10 db.

What does the term Hertz mean? Hertz or *Hz* is a unit of frequency equal to one cycle per second to describe sonic wave properties.

Multiples of hertz that are commonly known today are: the frequencies of radio and television waves which are measured in kilohertz (kHz), the speeds of computer chips are measured in megahertz (MHz) and gigahertz (GHz), and the frequencies of light waves are measured in terahertz (THz) as in microwave ovens, for example.

The term hertz is derived from the name of German physicist, Heinrich Rudolf Hertz (1857-1894), who proved that energy is transmitted through a vacuum by electromagnetic waves.

What is a wavelength? Sound can also be measured by the space occupied by each wave cycle in meters. The wavelength is the distance between identical points in the adjacent cycles of a waveform. Wavelength is also measured in relationship to a frequency. The higher the frequency signals, the shorter the wavelength.

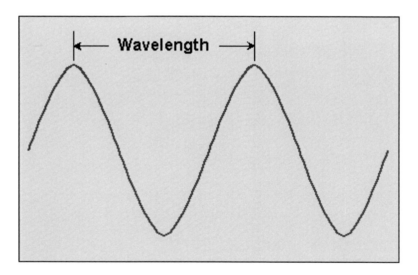

All of these aspects of sound are part of our environment. Low-volume (db) and non-jarring sounds (Hz) provide the most conducive atmosphere for animals. Reflective sounds from walls and speakers also have an affect on them, especially within closed environments.

The Hearing Ranges of Dogs, Cats and Horses

Dogs, cats and horses hearing are measured in decibels (volume) and frequencies (Hertz or cycles) and wavelengths.

A Human has a hearing range between:

64 -23,000 Hz

(at 4 dB for the best level)

Your Horse has a hearing range between:

55-33,500 Hz

(at 2 dB for the best level)

Your Dog has a hearing range between:

67-45,000 Hz

(at 8dB for the best level)

Your Cat has a hearing range between:

45-64,000 Hz

(at 8 dB for the best level)

Notice that the Hz numbers demonstrate a marked similarity between human and equine hearing range. Cats have an even higher and lower hearing range than dogs.

If a dog is sitting by a speaker on the floor and the bass frequencies go below 60 cycles per second or 60 Hz, the sound exerts pressure on the dog's middle and inner ear, which could be painful. The sound coming from the speaker manipulates the air, pushing it at a volume and frequency below the hearing range of the dog. This may subtly cause discomfort and an irate behavioral reaction. To understand how your pet feels such pressure, place your hand on the sound source of a radio or TV and you will feel the pressure of the sound against or within your hand.

What we know to date has been largely understood and discovered by animal behavior departments and acoustic science laboratories in universities around the world, particularly over the past five decades. Many years of intensive experiments and methodologies have been developed to achieve conclusive data. In addition, with the invention of analog and digital equipment and software, researchers can now determine and measure sound waves into the thousandths of sound bytes. A great amount of this information, in my estimation, is to be credited to the scientific accomplishments of Henry E. Heffner and Richye S. Heffner of the Laboratory of Comparative Hearing, Department of Psychology at University of Toledo Ohio whose research has been a major resource for this book. Heffner writes:

"There have been three main sources of selective pressure on the ability of animals to perceive sound (Masteron and Diamond, 1973). The first has been the need to detect a sound, an ability that enables an animal to determine the presence of sound-producing objects in its environment, which in most cases are other animals. The second has been the need to localize the source of a sound so that an animal can either approach or avoid the sound source. Finally, an animal must be able to identify the biological meaning or relevance of the sound so that it may respond appropriately to the sound source. Over the last decade, our knowledge of the auditory abilities of animals in general has been the object of study because it was necessary to determine the hearing abilities of large mammals in order to answer certain questions concerning the evolution of human hearing." H. E. Heffner, Farm Animals and the Environment. (pp.159-184). Wallingford UK: CAB International.

Using music to benefit animals in their environment is not a new concept. It has been documented that dairy cows produce more milk when listening to relaxing music. Researchers believe that farmers could get an extra pint from their charges by playing classical music. Psychologists Dr. Adrian North and Liam MacKenzie at the University of Leicester, UK played music of different tempos to herds of Friesian cattle. Beethoven's Pastoral Symphony resulted in greater milk production. When loud and rowdy music was played, there was no increase in milk yield. "Calming music can improve milk yield, probably because it reduces stress," said North and MacKenzie.

What is the difference between music for humans and music designed for pets?

In the pet industry today, quite a few music CDs have been produced especially for animals. This is a good thing as it affirms that musicians and pet owners understand the positive aspects of music for animals. The concept, however, must not be infused with entertainment for the pet owner if the goal is to encourage positive behavior in the pet's environment. Recorded music for humans has a broad range of frequencies with varying dynamics and volume levels. Music for human listening does not guarantee behavioral calm and a soothing environment for animals. The Relaxation Music Series is contoured specifically for these results. What makes the difference is to be able to control the volume levels by eliminating the ultra-high and sub-low frequencies. Information and research on the hearing ranges of dogs, cats and horses substantiates these criteria for this process. Good science combined with thoughtful recording techniques is what makes the difference in creating music capable of relaxing an animal. Though I am an advocate for all animals, my focus thus far has been on canine, feline and equine responses to music.

While composing, I place the music in the register or octave range best suited to the animal. The final stage of the production is to digitally position the frequency range of the music directly in the middle of their hearing comfort zone to avoid any extremes that would cause an animal stress or make them flee from their resting place.

There are four parts to the production process: composing, recording, mixing and mastering the music. One technique is to engineer the recording using only primary, secondary and third-order harmonics. Next, sub-low and ultra-high frequencies are intentionally eliminated from the mix to avoid jarring sound. The music undergoes a third process when it is compressed.

The fourth step is to master the whole CD for continuity of volume level. The end result is music contoured for your pet. When this music is playing, it will permeate the pet's environment and have a calming effect.

The sequence of the music is also designed to be musically active in the beginning before shifting into a long meditation-like section in the middle, and then gradually becoming more musically active towards the end. Putting the CD player on repeat makes the turn-around to the beginning without any sudden changes in dynamic levels. This design is incorporated in all of the Relaxation Music CDs.

You now know that dogs and cats can become agitated when subjected to very low and very high frequencies as well as high volume levels. It is not uncommon to hear stories of dogs running away from July 4th firework celebrations. As much as it is great fun to have your dog at a fireworks display, consider that for them, the experience is like having the sonic impact of a cannon firing just slightly above a person's head.

Once Relaxation Music for Dogs and Cats was completed, I was ready to test the product design. I took the music to veterinarians' offices, local rescue organizations and grooming businesses, and friends' homes where pets were present. Noting that the environments became calmer, I could see that dogs were resting within 5 to 7 minutes. Cats that were out of view in the home came into the room with the music and curled up to rest. Interestingly, the particular cats that I observed chose the sonic sweet spot in the room to sit. That is the spot where the sound image centers in the air. Rescued dogs at the kennel dimished their anxious barking. The recovery area at the veterinary hospital had a pleasant feel to it and the staff commented to me that it helped them feel calm as well.

Pet owners who played the music offered the most detailed results. "As my dogs and cats listened to the long, soft tones of the music I could see their bodies relax in a very short period of time. They remained content in their places until it was time to go out for a walk."

While visiting a friend's riding stable, I realized that I wanted to continue the CD series for equine well-being. Horses are such beautiful and sensitive animals that I saw the possibilities for music in their environment as well. With similar research and the same recording process, Relaxation Music for Horses for Equine Well-Being was completed and ready for a trial run to observe its effect on horses. Horse owners immediately understood the value and the possible uses of the product as many already play radios in their barns.

My observations were noted during grooming sessions, veterinary exams and while following horseshoers on their rounds. The music was placed close to the horses to help mask some of the sharp sounds, seeming to calm them. During barn time, the music was heard on a sound system broadcasting from each open end of the building. There was definitely less movement in the stalls while the music was playing..

There are several differences between equine music and the music for dogs and cats. One difference is that I put more rhythms in the compositions and fewer long tones that dogs and cats seem to respond to when they listen. Horse owners advised me before I began that their horses liked to listen to country music on the radio in the barn. I took their advice to heart and composed music with lilting rhythms and melodies.

Another difference is that *Relaxation Music for Dogs and Cats* is placed in a much higher register than the *Relaxation Music for Horses* CD. For horse listening comfort, I chose to place the range of the compositions in more of an alto register.

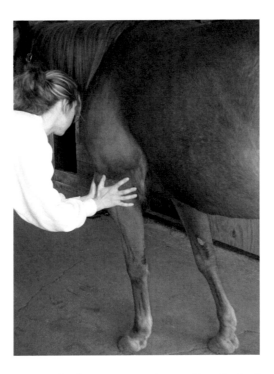

Like massage for humans, music can benefit the horse by
providing a tranquil acoustic environment.

How to Use Music for the Benefit of Your Pet

Now that you know that your pet's hearing capabilities are amazing, the next step is to learn how to use this knowledge to improve their behavior with controlled sound in the environment. The best-controlled sound we can offer them is the sonic field of music.

Many pet owners leave the TV, radio or sound system on while away from home, instinctively realizing that pets need the company of sound to fill their environment. Pet owners have told me that they have tried various kinds of music and discovered that a mix of classical and new age music has been effective in calming their pets.

At Home Alone / Barn Time

"I put music on before I leave and then my dogs settle right down. It is soothing and it helps cover some of the neighborhood noises."

When your pet is at home alone you can put the Relaxation Music for Dogs and Cats CD on repeat mode near where your pet is most likely to rest. It is best to have the music source at a level where the dog, cat or horse can feel the vibration of the music. The volume of the music is best at a moderate volume level.

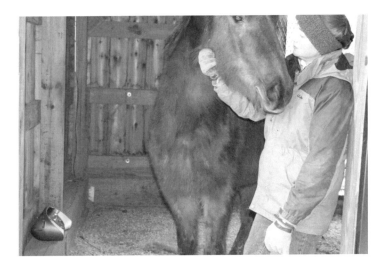

"The soft light sweetly melodic soundtracks create a tranquil acoustic environment, wherever it may be needed or wanted. Horses seem to enjoy and truly benefit from it."
Natural Horse Magazine

While Traveling/ Horse Trailers

" I can't believe the difference in Buddy's car behavior with the music playing. He used to jump on the seat nervously while I was driving. Now he lies down with his head on my hand which is on the stick shift."

" We travel in our motor home with 3 of our dogs and play the music many times. When we play it we note they yawn, relax more and often nap. The music has calmed all of us during our long trips."

Some horses display agitated behavior around their trailer, especially if they have had some trailer-related negative experience in the past. Playing music can mask common travel noises in transporting your horse or horses. Relaxation Music for Horses is specifically designed for these scenarios.

For Veterinary Visits and Post Surgery Environments

"The music is very soothing to our patients. Several anxious pets became more relaxed while listening to the music." Litchfield Veterinary Hospital, Connecticut

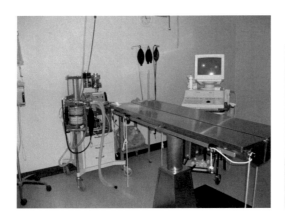

I am grateful to the staff of the Litchfield Veterinary Hospital for their care for Osborn, who inspired the CD Series. *Relaxation Music for Dogs and Cats* can now be heard playing for all the animals in the kennel, in the post surgery area and in the feline and canine areas.

Adoption Kennels and Rescue Organizations

The innocence of animals deserve our protection and care. Rescued animals can benefit from the soothing environment of music during their stay in animal welfare shelters.

Horse Rescue and Retirement Organizations

There are many dedicated organizations worldwide for abandoned, abused, neglected, or unwanted horses. Playing music for them in the stalls can help to calm and bring balance back to their lives.

Puppy and Kitten Training

Using music for training can be a gentle method to introduce your puppy to crate training and quiet time. When it is time for your puppy to quiet down, place a portable CD player near the crate and initiate playing the music. Repeat this method to help your puppy understand that it is time to be calm.

For kitten litter box training. After your kitten has been praised for going in the litter box spend a few minutes with the music playing while you give your kitten a nice treat. They will soon associate playing the music and treat with the positive behavior of using the litter box.

Masking Thunder Storms

While thunderstorms can occur at a high level of 110-115 dB, there are different behavioral theories as to whether or not pet owners should desensitize their pets to this experience. If your pet is simply too anxious to handle the ongoing thunderclaps, use the Relaxation Music to mask the sound of the storm. Bring the CD player to where your pet finds comfort. Play the music at a slightly higher volume than you would normally play it to fill the area with music. If you know the thunderstorm is approaching ahead of time, put the music on to settle the feeling of the environment.

Music for Grooming and Pet Sitting Businesses

*"For all our clients, music is part of their grooming session.
It settles-down the most anxious of our dog and cat clients."*

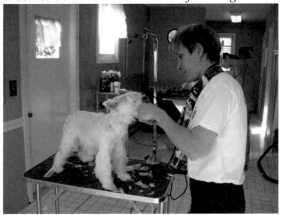

*"After a good exercise session, I bring the dogs in for
quiet- time with relaxation music to bring balance to their day."*

*"As a professional pet sitter, the music has become a valuable tool. The CD's
have relaxing and healing effects. I incorporate it into every single pet sitting assignment
and canine fitness programs."*

Stress and Separation Anxiety

Separation anxiety is the most common behavior problem when pets are left home alone. Having music on during the time that you are away is an easy and useful tool to help anxious pet behavior with positive results.

"I have a beautiful dog named Opal who I rescued last year and who happens to have serious separation anxiety. She had to be crate trained because my husband and I have come home to many messes, shoes chewed up, blinds torn down, pillow feathers thrown all around to name a few. When it's time to leave the house, I tell her to "kennel up" and she goes in, but when I shut the door she looks at me with those sad eyes and cries. Now, I have the CD playing in her room and I tell her to go in but she doesn't cry now! I even came back once to check on her, she was sleeping in the crate with the music playing softly!"

"I believe Relaxation Music for Dogs and Cats has a significant calming effect on our hospitalized patients. We have found it has helped to reduce their anxiety while away from their families." Dr. Laura Carey, Litchfield Veterinary Hospital

Music For Massage and Aqua Therapies

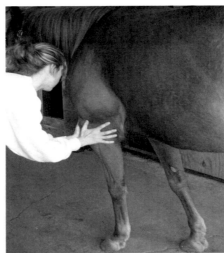

"Music vibrates their bodies on a cellular level. The music becomes part of the rhythm of the massage."

"The music sounds great to me and the pets! A nice relaxation tool while massaging pets or working with pets in the pool."

Music For Pets at the Office and Home Office

"The music is a gift for pets as an experience, not just for their ears but for their caregiver's hearts as well." Mary Pope Osborne, author of
The Magic Tree House Series with her dogs, Joey and Mr. Bezo.

"We found Scarlet as a kitten outside our office building, freezing and homeless. We have been her caring office family ever since."

Good for Pet Owners Too!

There is a secondary benefit to soothing music for your pet.

Music that has been processed by compressing sonic frequencies has a relaxing effect on humans as well. That is part of the magic! You and your pet can de-stress together just by sharing some quiet time with your best friend listening to music. We live in a fast moving world. If we feel it so do our pets because they care to share our lives so intimately with us.

Music was so soothing to my dog, Miles. No matter how much running around he did before it was time for me to do yoga, he always came to my yoga mat, found a spot and after listening to a few moments of the soothing music, he would invariably be totally relaxed, on his back, with his tummy exposed, legs up...in a deep sleep. Never failed! When he saw the yoga mat and the music, he ran immediately to his "spot" knowing it was our time to relax. Dr. Dale V. Atkins, PhD author of Sanity Savers: Tips for Women to Live a Balanced Life, Avon / HarperCollins Publisher

Relaxation Music for My Pet and Me is designed for people and their pets to enjoy a relaxed atmosphere together.

New Roles for Pets in the 21st Century

As we progress into the first decade of the 21st century, having pets in our homes are becoming an important part of people's lives. We know that the senses of dogs, cats and horses are much greater than ours. Perhaps we need them in our lives, to show us the appreciation of what we are missing in the moment, because we are thinking instead of using our noses. I once asked a wise friend "why do we love our pets so much and what is the need to touch them?" He said, "Because they are pure soul!"

The following are just some of the important ways in which animals participate in our lives today.

- Servicing people with physical disabilities
- Companions to assist the visually and hearing impaired
- As detectives to smell hidden dangers such as bombs
- For search and rescue
- Assisting archeologists on digs
- Visiting the elderly for companionship
- Visiting children in hospitals
- Children's reading programs; reading to the visiting dog
- Cats in businesses help to relax the employees
- Official greeters for businesses
- Therapeutic riding programs for young people
- Horses and dogs are official police
- Dogs detect human cancers
- Dolphins assist Naval missions
- Animal's behavior can predict earthquakes

FAQ

1.How do you know what animals like to hear?

Animals respond to frequency spectrums. With digital technologies and scientific studies in Universities on animal hearing capacities, research has been able to determine the specific range of frequencies of animals. An animal will stay near a source of music that has frequencies within their hearing range and move away from music that is jarring or extends outside their hearing capacities. Pet owners should make sure to turn OFF the subwoofers or turn down the excess bass, especially the louder they listen to music with their pets near by. Consider that an animal will "hear" ambient music approximately 3 times louder than we do or more.

2. What instruments do you use?

Relaxation Music for Dogs and Cats and *Relaxation Music for My Pet and Me* are CD's using synthesizer, music programs on computer and live recording for the orchestrations. The sustained long sounds of the synthesizer are most relaxing to dogs and cats. *Relaxation Music for Horses* and *For Pets and Pet Lovers Relaxation Music for the Holidays* consist of tracks that include the sounds from a synthesizer with the in-studio playing of my classical ten-string guitar. The good news is that the music can be composed on any instrument. Once the orchestrations are complete, it is the end process that fine tunes the listening comfort in regards to the CD production and the desired results. I have several software programs that graphically determine the frequency range that I have composed the music in. The final production phase is when I contour the "mastered CD" according to the frequency range. This guarantees the end result while centering the hearing range criteria. Each CD offers my musical expression and care which becomes a product for pet owners to use for the purpose of eliciting calm for the specific breed of animal in their environment.

3. Do you have certain pieces that you recommend for relaxing a pet and others that might be more stimulating, to encourage play?

The key to having your pet enjoy music is to limit the frequency spectrum and the volume. Use simple, melodious tracks like soft Classical, ecclesiastic music, Gregorian chants or New Age music, which is meant to soothe and calm. There is relatively little music production done expressly for the pet environment.

That is why I created the CD series. This is some of the only music in the world completely produced for the human AND animal sensitivities.

4. Is there a difference between music you would create for dogs and for cats or horses?

The hearing range of dogs and cats are relatively within the same range, though cats can hear a little lower and higher than dogs. *Relaxation Music for Dogs and Cats* has many successful responses from pet owners for both dogs and cats and many homes have both pets. Horses have a hearing range most closely related to humans. You can hear the differences in the recordings by comparison. The dog and cat CD's are placed in registers much higher than *Relaxation Music for Horses*. This CD is the first recording in this series where I have added my ten-string guitar. The range of a guitar is an instrument that fits well into the equine hearing range.

5. Do you have a CD for birds?

My husband and I are bird watchers and so my interest would be to compose music for them. Clearly birds *are* musicians. The investigations into their hearing ranges and responses are relatively a new scientific area.

6. How do you choose your track titles?

Through the process of each recording, I try to imagine what a dog, cat or horse would like to listen to. As a composer, putting the imagery of the scene in mind, is one of my greatest pleasures. I thoroughly enjoy instilling emotional energy into the music knowing that it will have a positive effect for our animal friends. The title of each track is a reflection of the imagery of the musical content. Each track title is my way of communicating with the pet owner of the musical direction of the music.

About Janet Marlow

Janet Marlow is one of the few artists in the world whose performances and recordings are acclaimed as one of the leading players, composers and arrangers on the ten-string guitar. Her performances have taken her around the world, which include venues such as the Lincoln Center, the Texaco Jazz Festival, Festival Estival De Paris, The Quick Center for the Arts, The Apollo, Carnegie Hall and the Blue Note in New York. Her virtuosity in BOTH classical and jazz musical forms has been acknowledged internationally as a soloist, with orchestras and with contemporary ensembles. She has composed for television documentaries; stage premieres in Asia and Europe and performs on screen in Woody Allen's Celebrity. Her playing on the ten-string is featured in the Sun Dance award winning film, *Swimmers.*

Born in London, Janet Marlow is the fifth generation of musicians. Classically trained as a violinist and pianist, she studied classical guitar with Maestro Andres Segovia in Spain and then became the protégé of Maestro Narciso Yepes, the innovator of the modern ten-string guitar.

Today, Janet's compassion for animals has led her to research the hearing senses, interpretive capacities and safe acoustic environments for animals, which developed the evolving series of *Relaxation Music for Dogs and Cats.*

Janet Marlow has also developed therapeutic music environments for animal massage entitled, *The Pet Owners' Massage Guide for Dogs and Cats DVD* guide. In 2006, *Relaxation Music for Horses for Equine Well-Being* and *For Pets and Pet Lovers Relaxation Music for the Holidays* were added to the CD Series.

The Magic of Music for Pets *Book* was a natural next step for Janet. The scientific research and multiple uses of the music described in this publication is Janet Marlow's interest to further the awareness of pet owner's and caregivers on the importance of understanding the hearing sensitivities of their pet for well-being in their environment.

Janet with Oliver

Music Catalogue

 Relaxation Music for Dogs and Cats CD

Soothing, Calming

 Relaxation Music for My Pet and Me CD

Relaxing, Soothing, Deep rest, Taking Time, Best Buddy, Dreams, Good Company, Time for a Walk

 For Pets and Pet Lovers Relaxation Music for the Holidays CD

Home Together, Family and Friends, Candles, Treats, Winter Walk, Stuffed Toys, Dreams Of Olde, Crystal Evening, A Favorite Place, Good Company, Peace On Earth

 Relaxation Music for Horses for Equine Well-Being CD

Free to Run, Morning Groom, On the Trail, Dreams of Fields, Desert Sunset, Stable Siesta, Ride for a Friend, Afternoon Trot, Hooves Grooves, Saddling Up

The Pet Owners Massage Guide for Dogs and Cats *DVD* demonstrates **The Bancroft School of Massage Therapy** techniques with the music of Janet Marlow's Relaxation Music for Dogs and Cats. Preserving health, preventing injury and by giving your pet the gift of your company through massage. Massage therapy techniques have been developed by The Small Animal Massage Certification Program at the Bancroft School of Massage Therapy in Worcester, Ma.

Janet Marlow Music LLC

www.musicforpetsandpeople.com

Janet Marlow Music LLC   PO Box 945 Litchfield, CT 06759   (860) 567-9217

info@musicforpetsandpeople.com

References

American Pet Products Manufacturers Association (2007) Industry trends and Statistics, <www.appma.org/press_industrytrends.as>

Heffner, H. E. and Heffner, R. S. (2007). Hearing ranges of laboratory animals. Journal of the American Association for Laboratory Animal Science, **46**, 11-13.

Heffner, H. E., & Heffner, R. S. (1992). Auditory perception. In C. Phillips and D. Piggins (Eds.), Farm Animals and the Environment. (pp.159-184). Wallingford UK: CAB International.

Heffner, H. E. (1998). Auditory awareness in animals. Applied Animal Behaviour Science, **57**, 259-268.

Johnson, H. Taylor (2006) The Art of Sound, Taylor Hohendahl Engineering, Jan. 2006 <www.theaudio.com>

Masteron, B. and Diamond, I.T. (1973) Hearing: Central neural mechanisms. In: Carterette, E.C. and Friedman, M.P. 9eds) Handbook of Perception, vol. 3 Biology of Perceptual Systems. Academic Press, New York, pp.407-448

Mattila, A.S. and Wirtz, J. (2001), Congruency of Scent and Music as a driver of In-Store Evaluations and Behavior, In: Journal of Retailing **77**, pp. 273-289.

Wolfe, J. (2007) What is a decibel? The University New South Wales, Sydney, Australia, Music Acoustics, <www.phys.unsw.edu.au>.

Wikipedia, the free encyclopedia (2007) Dog whistle, <en.wikipedia.org/wiki/Dog_whistle>

Photograph Credits

1. pg. 18, "Buddy", Stephen Rekas, Mel Bay Publications
   www.guitarsessions.com

2. pg. 20, Halide Caine, Connecticut Equine Massage
   www.ctequinemassage.com

3. pg. 22, Wendy and Russ Murdock, Spindle Brook Farm, LLC
   Litchfield, CT

4. pg. 23, "Libby", Nancy Stokes Litchfield Pet Supply, Litchfield, CT
   www.litchfieldpetsupply.com

5. Pg. 24, Litchfield Veterinary Hospital, Connecticut

6. pg. 25, Little Guild of St. Francis, Cornwall, CT
   www.littleguild.org

7. pg. 26, Pet Center LLC, Torrington, CT

8. pg. 28, Susan Begasse, Pet Aesthetics Salon and Boutique,
   Southbury, CT www.petaesthetics.com

9. pg. 28, Wendy Broeder, Peace of Mind Pet Care, Litchfield, CT

10. pg. 28, Holly Strom, Alpha Girl Pets, Stamford, CT www.alphagirlpets.com

11. pg. 29, "Collette" David and Barb Starbuck, New Jersey

12. pg. 30, Pamela Holick, Hand Made Healing Massage Therapy
    New Milford, CT www.handmadehealing.com

13. pg. 30, Pamela Tewes, AquaDogFitness, Waltham, Ma.
    www.aquadogfitness.com

14. pg. 31, "Joey and Mr. Bezo", Mary Pope Osborne,
    Author of The Magic Tree House Series

15. pg. 31, "Scarlet" Mike Moore and Alan Brennan at O & G
    Industries, CT

16. FAQ Interview questions from Animal Wellness Magazine, Nov/Dec Issue
    www.animalwellnessmagazine.com